MR. MEN
Happy Fun

Roger Hargreaves

In these stories you will meet:

Mr Happy   Mr Grumble

Mr Strong

EGMONT

EGMONT
We bring stories to life

Book Band: Red

MR. MEN   LITTLE MISS

MR.MEN™ LITTLE MISS™ © THOIP (a SANRIO company)

Happy Fun © 2016 THOIP (a SANRIO company)
Printed and published under licence from Price Stern Sloan, Inc., Los Angeles.
Published in Great Britain by Egmont UK Limited
The Yellow Building, 1 Nicholas Road, London, W11 4AN

ISBN 978 1 4052 8268 0
63469/1
Printed in Singapore

Illustrated by Adam Hargreaves
Series and book banding consultant: Nikki Gamble

Written by Jane Riordan
Designed by Cassie Benjamin

MIX
Paper
FSC   FSC® C018306

Happy Fun

This is Mr Happy.

Hello, Mr Happy.

This is Happyland.
In Happyland the dogs
are happy.

In Happyland the fish
are happy.

But Mr Grumble was not happy.

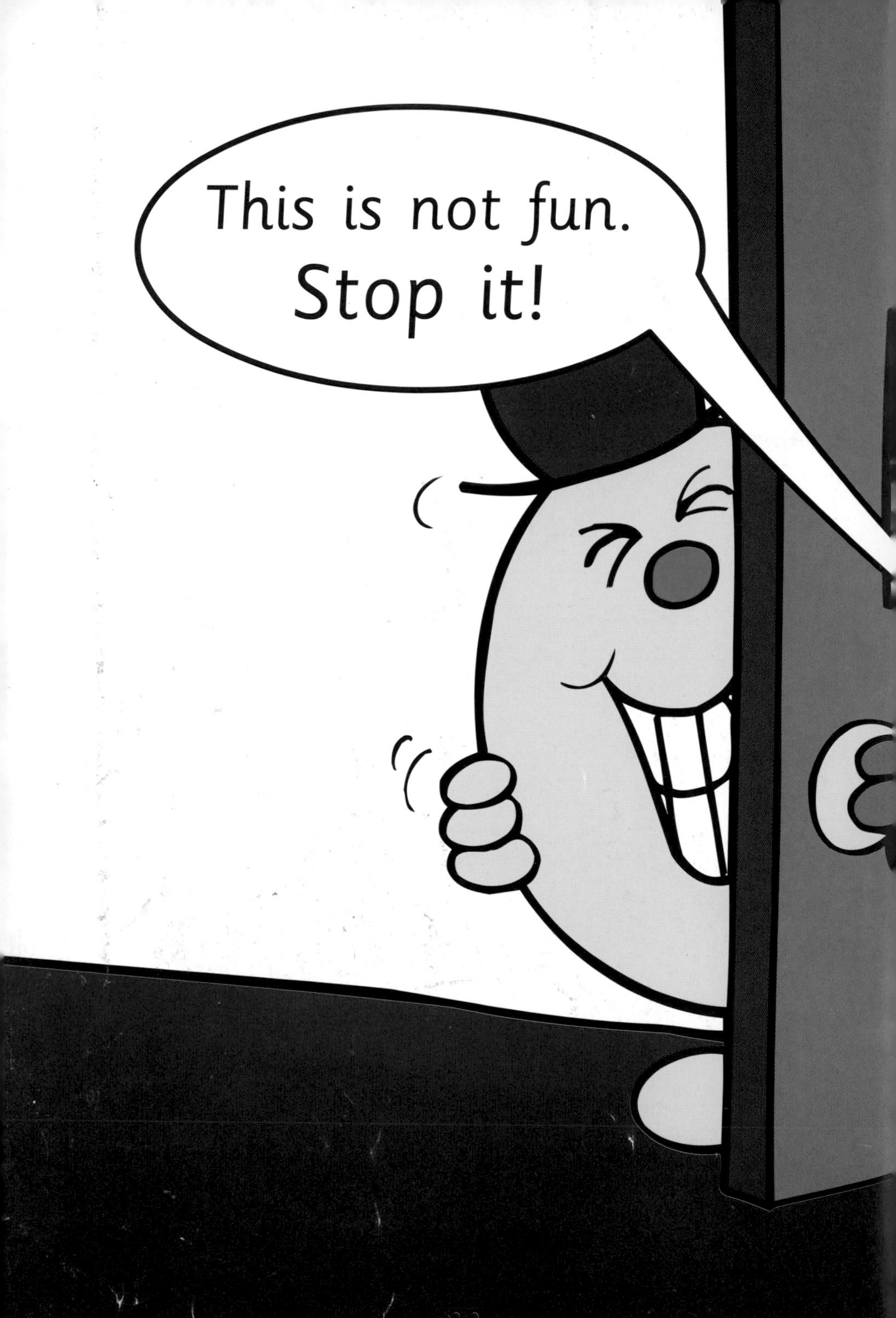
This is not fun.
Stop it!

Mr Grumble is happy
not to have fun!
Goodbye,
Mr Happy!

Goodbye,
Mr Grumble!

This is Mr Strong.

Hello, Mr Strong.

Mr Strong is strong.

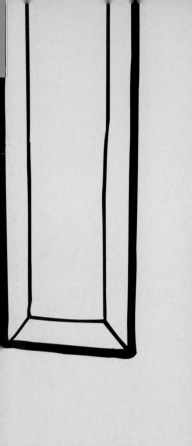

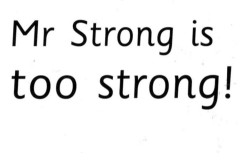

Mr Strong is too strong!

Mr Strong went out.

It was wet.

It was too wet.

So Strong

Follow the lines to help Mr Strong carry all the animals back to their homes.

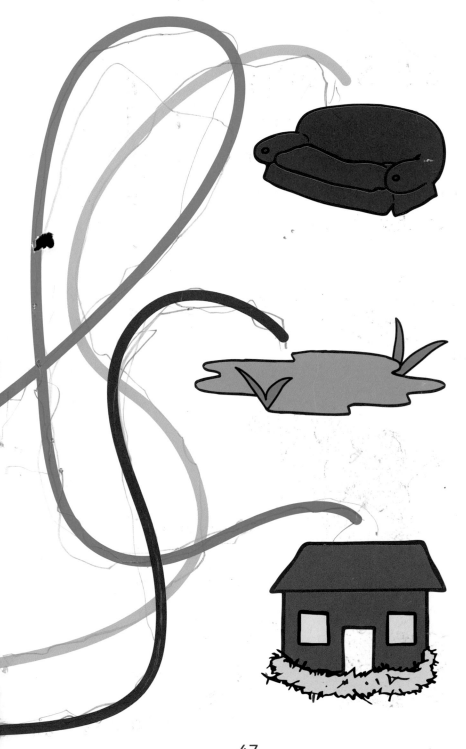

Happy or Sad?

Look at Mr Happy's friends.
Point to all the happy friends.
Now point to all the sad friends.

Read these words:

happy

sad